ISBN 978-0-266-76727-5
PIBN 10886762

MONTANA
FISH AND GAME
NOTES

PAUL MACLEAN, EDITOR

VOL. I   FEBRUARY ' 36   NO. II

This bulletin is edited monthly in the offices
of the Montana Fish and Game Commission, Helena,
Montana, and is published in the interest of sportsmen
and conservationists and the field force and employes
of the Department. Material used in the bulletin is
privileged matter and may be re-printed if proper
credit is given to this publication.

SPORTSMEN'S CLUBS OF MONTANA

ASKED TO COOPERATE

by

Kenneth F. MacDonald
State Fish and Game Warden

The backbone of the Fish and Game Commission is the
group of individuals who maintain the department through the
purchase of fishing and hunting licenses. With from eighty
to ninety thousand in Montana interested in the same general
hobby, it is necessary that some opportunity be afforded
whereby they may meet and discuss certain phases of the
hobby as only hobbyists can, and this opportunity is pro-
vided in the local Rod and Gun clubs or sportsmen's
associations where each is given free rein in voicing any
idea relating to fish and game.

As is characteristic of all sportsmen's meetings,
the presiding officer has great difficulty in keeping the
meeting in hand, due to one or another wishing to tell in
minute detail of a certain fishing or hunting trip which
to that individual far surpasses anything of its nature in
this or past generations. Each club or association has the
characteristic groups of bait fishermen, fly fishermen,

(1)

duck, upland bird and big game hunters and trappers. The
fisherman is little interested in the duck hunter's story
of how the dog retrieved the duck in icy waters and against
the greatest odds, and the duck hunter is equally dis-
interested in listening to an angler's account of landing
the fighting rainbow with every possible hazard to be
overcome.

With this in mind--and it is universal in each and
every club--it is suggested that such eagerness be harnessed
and the energy directed towards a gainful end.

The Fish and Game Commission
is charged with the responsibility of administering the
affairs of the department to
the very best interests of the
sportsmen. It is a mighty
large responsibility with the
multitude of problems and
ideas, and the commission wel-
comes suggestions or
recommendations from the
sportsmen; in fact, solicits
them. In many cases, it is
noted that an attitude of "let George do it" prevails in the
club when there is any work to be done and in practically
each club is to be found the characteristic group of
"willing horses" who accept the work of the organization and
the balance of the membership continues to lend only a
limited amount of moral support.

Would it not serve to enliven the interest in the club
and result in more intelligent and useful recommendations,
if each organization had committees appointed the early part
of each year for the purpose of studying particular phases
of the sport and submitting the report at a general meeting
to be acted upon and forwarded to the Fish and Game Commission
for its consideration?

All too often suggestions or recommendations are made
without proper background. If a committee of three, five or
seven be appointed on the fisheries section and delegated to
make observations and studies of all general factors and
conditions relating to this phase during the season in their
particular district, another committee to study the Chinese
pheasant and Hungarian partridge condition, another to
study native upland birds, another elk, another deer,
trapping and so on, it would result in a more comprehensive
study and consideration of conditions and ultimately result
in a decided improvement generally in the fish and game of
that particular section. It would tend to discourage the
snap judgment of certain individuals who are absolutely sin-
cere in the belief that their solution is the proper one, but

(2)

whi¢h will be found to fall far short of b¢ing such when all angles are considered.

In many sections certain species of birds are not doing so well as they should. There is a reason for this and a committee of three or five particularly interested in that part of the sport would enjoy studying the problem and be much more apt to reach a solution than a committee without the proper interest. And so it is with each and every species of fish and game. The revenue of the department will not support the employment of research men to study the many problems. The deputies are not permitted time to give proper study to all of these problems, nor are the fish culturists or the game farm employees, but each and every employee of the department will be glad to assist any committee in every way possible--furnish complete and accurate figures and number and species of fish or birds liberated in any particular locality. By assembling all facts and data, a reasonable and intelligent report on their findings and observations would result. This plan would require no extra work on the part of a sportsman interested in a certain problem. It would, on the other hand, tend to increase his interest with a resultant improvement or conservation of his favorite species of fish or game, would develop a new interest in the club's activities and make possible a better administration of fish and game in the state.

ADVICE GIVEN TO MINNOW

FISHERMEN

A. C. (Andy-Told-It) Baumgartner of Great Falls, member of the State Fish and Game Commission, is one fisherman who knows problems of sportsmen, particularly in the fishing field. At the January meeting of the commission he recommended that some action be taken in advising minnow fishermen not to dump their live bait back into the stream following their trips.

Commissioner Baumgartner said that a majority of the live minnow bait used consisted of small suckers. Although he does not countenance the use of sucker minnows as bait, he does contend that they should be properly disposed of in order to eliminate any possibility of this scavenger fish type getting a start in any game fish stream.

SPORTY MONTANA GRAYLING IS

STAGING A "COMEBACK"

by

Elmer G. Phillips
Superintendent of Fisheries

Exquisitely colored, graceful in action, shapely in form and a spirited fighter, the Mentana grayling is the delight of sportsmon.

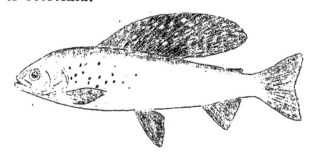

The grayling is very selective in its habitat and the planting of this species in new environment has been attended with much difficulty. It prefers the clear, cool, swift streams with gravel beds. Streams strewn with rocks and boulders are not to its liking, although it will enter them in search of food, for which it has been known to travel long distances. They are very selective in their food and the most specialized of fresh water fishes.

They normally spewn in April in streams having a temperature range between 50 degrees and 60 degrees Fahrenheit. The eggs are about one-eighth inch in diameter, pale yellow when first taken, adhesive and semi-buoyant. The eyes, small gilt specks with a tiny black spot, appear in from three to six days and hatch in fourteen to seventeen days in water temperature of approximately 50 degrees Fahrenheit.

Since the time of their introduction into Montana fairly efficient methods of incubation have been devised, and from which consistently good hatches are devised. The yolk sac of the eggs is quite small and is usually absorbed in less than a week after hatching. The young grayling are then hardly half an inch long, and move about continually in search of food. It has always boen necessary to plant the fry immediately after they absorb the egg sac, due to the inability of fish culturists to find a food which could be taken by these minute fish. The planting was always

(4)

carried on with a great degree of uncertainty as to the
results that would be accomplished and resolved entirely
into a trial and error procedure, with the errors over-
balancing the other side of the ledger by a heavy margin.

Many attempts and theories were made and tried to
rear these fish from the fry to the fingerling stage. A
large variety of foods were used in the experiments, but all
ended with very indifferent success and falling far short
of what could be called successful fish culture. In the
meantime, this beautiful fish was slowly vanishing and all
indications pointed to its ultimate extinction unless the
problem of successful propagation was soon solved.

This problem again was attacked by the personnel of
the Montana State Hatchery at Libby, Montana, in the spring
of 1935. As there was no equipment at the Libby station
for incubation, the eggs were hatched at the Somers station,
and the fry transported to the Libby Hatchery, where they
were placed in the standard troughs which are supplied with
a very pure spring water, at a constant temperature of 46
degrees Fahrenheit.

Prior to this, much investigation and preparation
had been carried on in an attempt to guarantee the success
of this experiment. A lake
was selected which was known
to consistently maintain a
relatively high daphnia con-
tent, and to which access
could be had by truck, and at
the same time be within reasonable distance of the
hatchery. The lake selected
is at the present time used
as a State spawning station
for eastern brook, and no
fishing is permitted therein.
It is approximately one and
one-half miles long, and
one-half mile wide, with a maximum depth of one hundred and
fifty feet and almost its entire area and depth contain a
heavy culture of daphnia.

A net for the capture of these specimens in large quan-
tities was devised, and is towed behind a small boat powered
with an outboard motor. A five minute tow with this net
yields approximately one gallon of these organisms. These
minute organisms are segregated by an intricate process and
the little grayling have no difficulty in capturing them.
They are held on this diet for the first two months. At the
end of this period a liver and salmon egg diet was substituted
and in a few days they were taking liver almost as greedily
as they had taken the daphnia.

An accurate check of the loss has been kept and,up to
date, which represents an eight months period,we have a
ninety-five and nine-tenths percent survival. This compares
very favorably with the trout culture carried on at that
station, and this spring will mark Montana's first ambitious
step into the field of grayling culture. It is no longer
an uncertain experiment, our food supply is almost unlimited,
and the methods involved in collecting it are neither com-
plicated nor costly. In fact it has been fed quite
extensively to the trout fry at that station as the cost of
gathering is found to be much less than the current price
paid for fresh liver or other food.

Our program for this year calls for the propagation and
liberation of at least one million fingerling Grayling to be
distributed in waters over the state which have been found
by observation and investigation to be best suited for the
introduction of this species, and we make the prediction
with all sincerity that it will be possible within a few
years for the angler to venture forth and again lure to the
well-cast fly that most beautiful of all fish - The Montana
Grayling.

SOCKEYE..............DRAMA

Sockeye salmon, a bone of contention to some members of
the angling population, do their part and do it mightily, at
least in the one portion of the state where they have made
their home.

Not only that but they provide drama, according to
J. J. Johnsrud, caretaker of the biological station at Yellow
Bay, near Bigfork, in the Flathead region.

The following inspired letter was written to the Fish
and Game Department,and it speaks for itself:

"On October 25, 1935, the sockeye salmon came into
Yellow Bay, perhaps as many as 700,000 of them. They stayed
for a few hours and went away again. On October 28 they
came back to take possession of the bay - to drive out the
other fishes, their enemies, and prepard their spawning beds.
So they bit Mr. Sucker in the tail and Mr. Squawfish in the
belly and large schools of them chased Mr. Bulltrout for a
quarter of a mile or more south around the bend. On the 2nd
day of November, I found six dead, three of them bulltrout,
two suckers and one large squawfish. The battle had been too

(6)

much for them. Their wounds were so deep and many that they did not survive.

"The sockeye salmon is well organized; they do team work and fight in squads or platoons. The big fellow with the hump on his back is the first in battle with his sharp saw teeth when some fish attempts to rob their spawning beds.

"Nearly a hundred tons of salmon were fished out of Yellow Bay this season. There are some people who do not like the sockeye but there seems to be plenty who like them. We have registered cars of fishermen from every county in Montana and from nearly every state in the union. Many Canadian cars were seen here in November and December.

"The sockeye salmon dies shortly after spawning, so the days of the 700,000 are numbered. The bottom of the bay is now strewn with the dead. A thirty-mile gale may come at any time and rock them from the bottom and toss them on the shore. The sea gulls are here waiting to have their feast. When they have scattered the bones of the dead, they will again be winging their way down the Columbia to the Pacific, and this is just one of the yearly dramas played at Yellow Bay."

THAR'S GOLD IN THEM

THAR ANIMALS

Montana's wealth in fur-bearing animals has never been determined, yet some inkling of it can be ascertained through the number of trapping permits issued by the State Fish and Game Commission.

Although the 1935-36 season does not expire until April 15, the game department has issued to date 390 regular trapping licenses at the required fee of ten dollars per license, and some 350 land owners' trapping licenses at one dollar per license. These licenses are scattered over the rich game areas of Montana and it is logical to assume that their rewards are manifold. The commission hopes some time to devise a system whereby the approximate value of fur-bearing animals may be determined.

The Fish and Game Department issues this one-dollar land owner's trapping license which entitles a holder to trap fur-bearing animals upon his own land only. When making application for this license it is necessary to state the legal description of the land owned or leased by the applicant. No beaver may be taken under this permit, as special permits are issued in that respect.

BUCK LAW MEETING WITH

HEARTY APPROVAL

The so-called buck law in Montana, which the past season went into effect in all game areas in the state with two small exceptions, is meeting with the hearty approval of sportsmen and many organizations are commencing a movement to have the same policy continued this coming season.

Two of the outstanding sportsmen's clubs in Montana already have gone on record as favoring it. They are the Lewistown Rod and Gun Club and the Paradise Rod and Gun Club.

In a letter to the state fish and game warden the Lewistown club said in part: "You may be sure big game hunters of central Montana will strenuously oppose any modification of the present law to permit indiscriminate shooting of deer regardless of sex. Members of our organization and sportsmen in this vicinity have too much visible evidence of the success of the law in this part of the state to doubt for a moment its efficiency.."

C. D. Thaxton, secretary of the Paradise Rod and Gun Club, wrote the state warden in regard to action taken by the organization at its last meeting at Thompson Falls. One of the resolutions passed was "that there be a continuation of the buck law in Sanders county for the next season, and with the same dates as during the past season."

Other clubs in the state are of the same opinion generally, and the state fish and game department expects almost 100 percent cooperation in making the law a popular one. Records of the department, disclosed by the return of big game tags, indicate that Montana hunters enjoyed a sporty year under the buck law. Tags on file show that hunters brought down a total of 2,270 buck deer - good enough for any state.

DEATH TO.............MAGPIES!

BANG!

Sportsmen's organizations have launched during the recent years a state-wide campaign against the magpie, this wary feathered scavenger of the skies, this destroyer of song birds.

Incidently, the Fish and Game Commission is supporting this movement, including a campaign to control coyotes. It this year has sent out to all deputy game wardens poison to bo distributed and utilized in the control of these two outstanding game killers of the land and air. This poison is being distributed by the deputies to responsible parties and organizations with full instructions as to its use.

Deputy wardens have been advised to be cautious, to use care and to supervise the utilization of the poison. All "baits" will be removed by the wardens before the song birds start their migration from the south.

A bulletin has been issued to all deputy wardens instructing them as to the safe methods in using the poison. This bulletin explains in detail "destroying magpie nests", "poisoning", "carrion stations", "suet baits" and "grain baits".

The bulletin carries this reminder: "CAUTION: Keep all surplus poison and poison containers plainly labelled and out of reach of irresponsible persons and domestic animals.."

When sportsmen's clubs start swinging their shot guns to their shoulders against the magpie this year, they should remember that the Fish and Game Commission is attempting to do its part in eliminating this feathered beast.

ON LEAVE

Tom Peasley, veteran game warden for the department, was granted a leave of absence for one year at the January meeting of the commission. The commission hopes that he will return to his duties at the expiration of the year.

FISH SURVEY PLANNED THIS

SPRING IN "NEW" AREA

Montana has a new fish and game area, opened up by the Red Lodge-Cooke City highway, and the Fish and Game Commission through its fisheries division is planning a comprehensive survey of that great rugged territory this spring so that the streams, lakes and other waters may be scientifically stocked with game fish.

Early this spring E. G. Phillips, Superintendent of Fisheries, will make a pack trip through that country to obtain definite data concerning the planting of fish. The lakes, being in a high altitude, constitute a peculiar problem. The fisheries department will have to take that into consideration, also the amount of feed available at each particular place, the growing time of the feed, and make plans for the introduction of the most suitable species of game fish to fit conditions.

It is a magnificent area and many of the streams and rivers and lakes abound with fish life. There are eastern brook trout, silver salmon, rainbow and natives ready to meet the coming of any sportsmen.

Last year the Fish and Game Commission commenced initial plans to stock the virgin waters in that great natural park of Montana. California golden trout and albino trout were packed into the hidden recesses of that alluring, yet unpenetrable area. As a result hitherto unidentified lakes now have names. They are Golden and Albino lakes.

Following the survey to be conducted this spring by Superintendent Phillips, a plan will be mapped out whereby the entire region will be stocked according to the most modern and scientific methods known to fishdom.

FIRST SUBSCRIBER

L. Anspach, 311 South 31st St., Billings, was the first to make application for a subscription to "Fish and Game Notes". The commission hopes that within the next few months other interested sportsmen in Montana will help out in this enterprise. It already has received the backing of many sportsmen's organizations. It is a magazine primarily designed for sportsmen.

ELK REDUCTION OF NORTHERN

HERD NECESSARY STEP

Preserve and protect all wild life, both animal and forage!

That was the policy upon which our National Parks progressed. It was under this protection that game increased and great herds of elk and deer expanded.

Many sportsmen have wondered why each year the Commission calls for a reduction in herds, particularly in the northern elk herd which summers within the bountiful confines of Yellowstone National Park. During the past few years it has been necessary to limit this splendid, glamorous herd to the extent of 3000 head.

There must be a balance between the organic and inorganic - the oldest law of nature. There must be a balance between the number of elk and the amount of grazing land. In the northern herd this balance has been upset; the elk have been increasing beyond their grazing limitations.

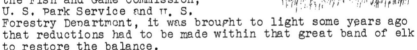

A thorough comprehensive study of the elk situation in Yellowstone National Park was conducted by Bill Rush, nationally-known game expert, and with the cooperation of the Fish and Game Commission, U. S. Park Service and U. S. Forestry Department, it was brought to light some years ago that reductions had to be made within that great band of elk to restore the balance.

In order that the elk could be made available to hunters on the outside of the park, the Fish and Game Commission consulted old employees of the department and other game agencies interested in the park policy of reduction and this season decided to close the old "firing line" and to extend the closed area to its present boundaries.

Reports received since the change in weather are that everything is satisfactory, both to the hunters and to those interested in the welfare of the herd. The elimination of the old firing line and the creation of the new was a move on the part of the commission to do away with "unsportsmanlike slaughter."

(11)

hooting of elk in Park county thus is made "more
unt". To date approximately 1500 elk have been
by hunters. The commission desires, as well as do
fficials, that Mentana sportsmen may reduce the herd
00 head. With the season extended to March 1 this
ay be reached. Otherwise, park officials say, live
ill have to be transplanted or slaughtered and the
distributed through various channels.

---

46 GAME AND FISH ARRESTS

MADE IN JANUARY

There were 46 game violation arrests made by the
ment during January, according to a tabulation made
F. Chartrand, chief deputy.

large number of the violations were in connection
he illegal hunting and shooting of elk. In many
ces fines were imposed by the presiding justices of
although there were several cases where defendants
eund not guilty.

One deputy game warden, in reporting a trial wherein
efendant was charged with shooting elk in a closed area
in Park county and found not
guilty, wrote: "The trial
evidently was considered a joke."

It is time the entire state of
Montana, including its justice
courts, do not consider violations of game laws "a joke".

The following shows the game
law violations for January:

Failing to fill out game tags, two; fishing without a
se , four; shooting elk before 8 a. m. in Park county,
; shooting more than one elk, two; possession of elk
roperly tagged, one; killing and possessing more than
lk, one; illegal ice fishing, one; fishing with more
one rod and line, ten; alien gun law, one; killing elk
osed area, three; unlawfully killing antelope, one;
al possession of a portion of a deer and three deer
, one; illegal possession of elk, one; possession of
ged elk; one; unlawfully tagging elk with another
l's tag; one; trapping fur-bearing animals without a
se, one; unlawful possession of mink skins, one;

(12)

killing three deer out of season, one; killing two deer
out of season, one; illegal possession of deer meat,
illegal possession of beaver skins and illegal possession
of muskrat and red fox skins, one; shooting from public
highway, three; and killing deer out of season, one.

UNIQUE...............IF TRUE

Years ago, near the State Penitentiary, a certain
deputy game warden encountered a problem that even the
Attorney General or Blackstone himself could not have
solved. The story goes that a group of prisoners detailed
to road work was near a choice fishing stream which had
been closed by order of the Fish and Game Department.

In the group there were a few followers of Isaac
Walton who had fallen from the "straight and narrow" but
still were followers of that great leader of the angling
fraternity.

In their spare moments the prisoners improvised fishing
rods and other equipment. At any rate, while they were
supposed to be constructing roads and literally making
"little ones out of big ones", they sauntered away with
their fishing stuff and tossed a hook into the favored but
closed stream nearby. A deputy game warden surprised them
as they were enjoying this sport with the fighting, ravenous
and plentiful trout abounding in the stream.

"You are under arrest", the deputy game warden said,
"and I'll have to take you to jail."

"You can't arrest us", they said in chorus, as they
continued to cast their lines upon the enticing riffles of
the closed waters.

"And why not?" inquired the deputy game warden,
disclosing his badge.

"Because we are already in prison", the spokesman said
as a two-pound Rainbow struck his prison-made hook.

The outcome was that the warden of the penitentiary
was called upon to admonish his enthusiastic convict fishermen.

Automobiles in Montana yearly account for the loss of
untold thousands of game birds.

(13)

SPORTSMEN URGED TO BE AWARE

OF STREAM POLLUTION

Although there are no acute situations in Montana at the
present time, sportsmen should be aware of the fact that there
are many possibilities of stream pollution.

Figures given out by Dr. W. F. Cogswell, Secretary of the
Board of Health, disclose that there are approximately 200
industrial sites in the state that might result in the pollution
of streams, which would be detrimental not only to human but
fish life as well.

There is only one bad situation in the state at the present
time, according to the officials of the State Board of Health,
and that is Milk River. The health department has jurisdiction
only over waters which are used for domestic purposes and has
no supervisory capacity over any streams that are not used as
supplies for municipalities. There is no question in the minds
of the health officials that the situation in Milk River,
occasioned by apparent pollution from Havre's sewage disposal
system, has affected game fish in that river. It is an old fight
with the Board of Health, one that goes back 22 years, but it is
the hope of the State Board that the situation will be solved
soon.

Stream pollution in Montana appears only in isolated
instances, but sportsmen should be aware of the situation and
whenever it occurs, should take such action as would be necessary
to curb and eliminate the source of contamination.

Industries in Montana have been cooperating to the fullest
degree in preventing pollution and are fully alive to its menace.
The waste from industrial activities is being studied so that
sanitary disposal will result. Many of the industries are constructing settling basins so that through sedimentation the
streams are kept free from possible contamination. Sportsmen
should hope that this policy will be maintained and that tech-
nical experts should be employed by such industries to study
and consider ways and means of effecting a clean, wholesome
and unpolluted disposal of waste products.

At the same time, sportsmen should remember, as the State
Board of Health points out, that there are approximately 200
industrial sites in Montana where stream pollution is possible.

(14)

MONTANA STATE FISH AND GAME DEPARTMENT

Commissioners

Ray G. Lowe, Chairman, Glendive

W. C. Keil, Billings   J. J. Harper, Anaconda
P. G. Gutensohn, Whitefish   A. C. Baumgartner, Grea

Kenneth F. MacDonald, State Fish and Game Warden

STATE FISH AND GAME WARDEN'S OFFICE STAFF
J. H. Chartrand, Chief Deputy   Nellie Raw, Secretary
William H. Voorhies, Cashier   Gertrude Simon, Stenog
Mary Walker, Stenographer

REGULAR DEPUTY GAME WARDENS
L. C. Clark, Havre   Frank Marshall, Bozeman
Harry Cosner, Malta   Bruce Neal, Augusta
Elmer DeGolier, Polson   A. A. O'Claire, Kalispe
W. J. Dorrington, Libby   Fred E. Pilling, Valier
W. A. Hill, Great Falls   Chas. R. Price, Dillon
A. T. Holmes, Billings   H. C. Sailor, Absarokee
Wm. Ray Kohls, Ennis   Frank Starina, Hardin
E. M. Krost, Missoula   Fred T. Staunton, Livin
J. P. McCaffery, Anaconda   J. A. Weaver, Lewistown

SPECIAL DEPUTY GAME WARDENS
H. B. Ives, Butte   George Muxlow, Glendive
John Iwen, Bainville   Len. J. Rensch, Miles C
Louis Miller, Harlowton   A. D. Roushar, Helena
Harry N. Mergan, Ovando   Dale T. Shook, Plains

FISHERIES DIVISION
Elmer G. Phillips, Superintendent, State Fisher
Ann Crimmins, Stenographer

FISH HATCHERIES
Anaconda, A. G. Stubblefield, Foreman
Big Timber, J. W. Schofield, Foreman
Daly (Hamilton), Melvin Larson, Foreman
Emigrant, Fred R. Real, Foreman
Great Falls, Leo Gilroy, Foreman
Lewistown, Iver Hoglund, Foreman
Libby, John P. Sheehan, Foreman
Ovando, George Miller, Foreman
Philipsburg (Rock Creek) John LaSalle, Foreman
Polson (Station Creek), O. W. Link, Foreman
Red Lodge, Ross Snyder, Foreman
Somers, J. Paul Campbell, Foreman
POND CULTURAL STATION
Eli Melton, Foreman, Miles City

STATE GAME FARM
J. F. Hendricks, Superintendent, Warm Springs

9 780266 767275